Jingle Bells

Dashing through the snow
    In a one horse open sleigh,
O'er the fields we go,
    Laughing all the way.

Bells on bobtail ring,
    Making spirits bright,
What fun is it to ride and sing
    A sleighing song to-night.

Oh! Jingle bells! Jingle bells!
    Jingle all the way!
Oh, what fun it is to ride
    In a one horse open sleigh, hey!

Jingle bells! Jingle bells!
    Jingle all the way!
Oh, what fun it is to ride
    In a one horse open sleigh! Hey!

THE PERFECT TREE

and Favorite Christmas Carols

Illustrated by
Christopher Bivins

Story by
Thomas Bivins

The Unicorn Publishing House
New Jersey

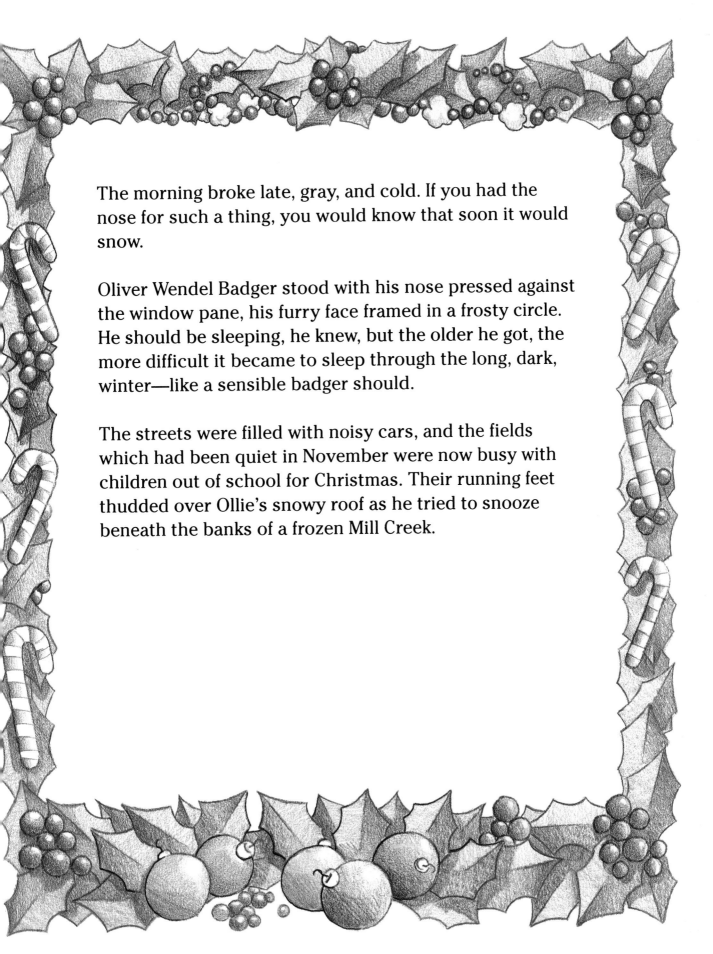

The morning broke late, gray, and cold. If you had the nose for such a thing, you would know that soon it would snow.

Oliver Wendel Badger stood with his nose pressed against the window pane, his furry face framed in a frosty circle. He should be sleeping, he knew, but the older he got, the more difficult it became to sleep through the long, dark, winter—like a sensible badger should.

The streets were filled with noisy cars, and the fields which had been quiet in November were now busy with children out of school for Christmas. Their running feet thudded over Ollie's snowy roof as he tried to snooze beneath the banks of a frozen Mill Creek.

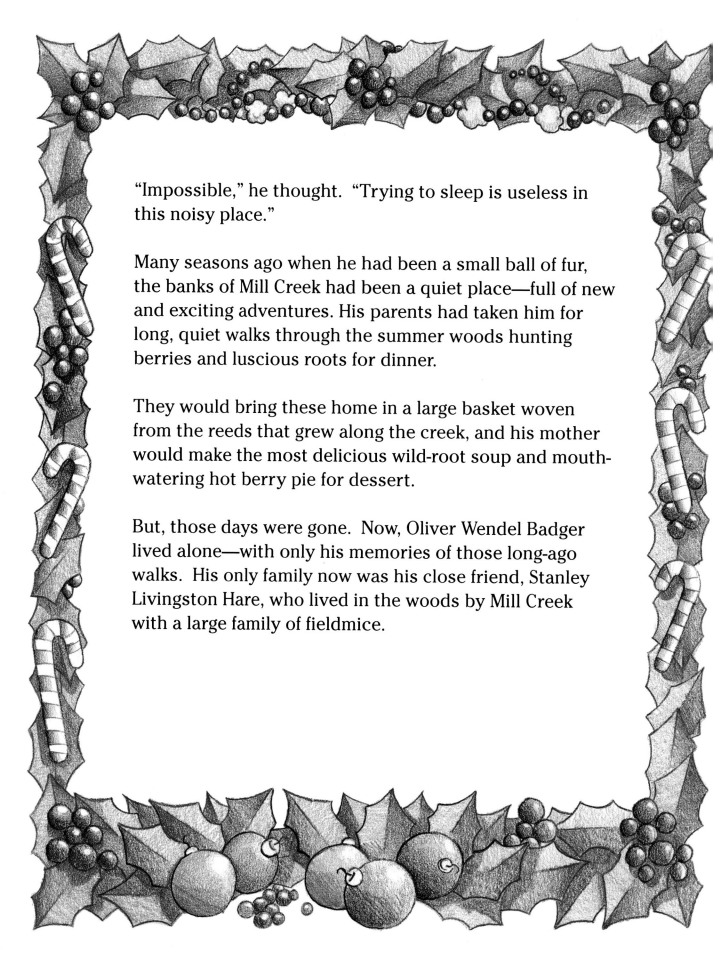

"Impossible," he thought. "Trying to sleep is useless in this noisy place."

Many seasons ago when he had been a small ball of fur, the banks of Mill Creek had been a quiet place—full of new and exciting adventures. His parents had taken him for long, quiet walks through the summer woods hunting berries and luscious roots for dinner.

They would bring these home in a large basket woven from the reeds that grew along the creek, and his mother would make the most delicious wild-root soup and mouth-watering hot berry pie for dessert.

But, those days were gone. Now, Oliver Wendel Badger lived alone—with only his memories of those long-ago walks. His only family now was his close friend, Stanley Livingston Hare, who lived in the woods by Mill Creek with a large family of fieldmice.

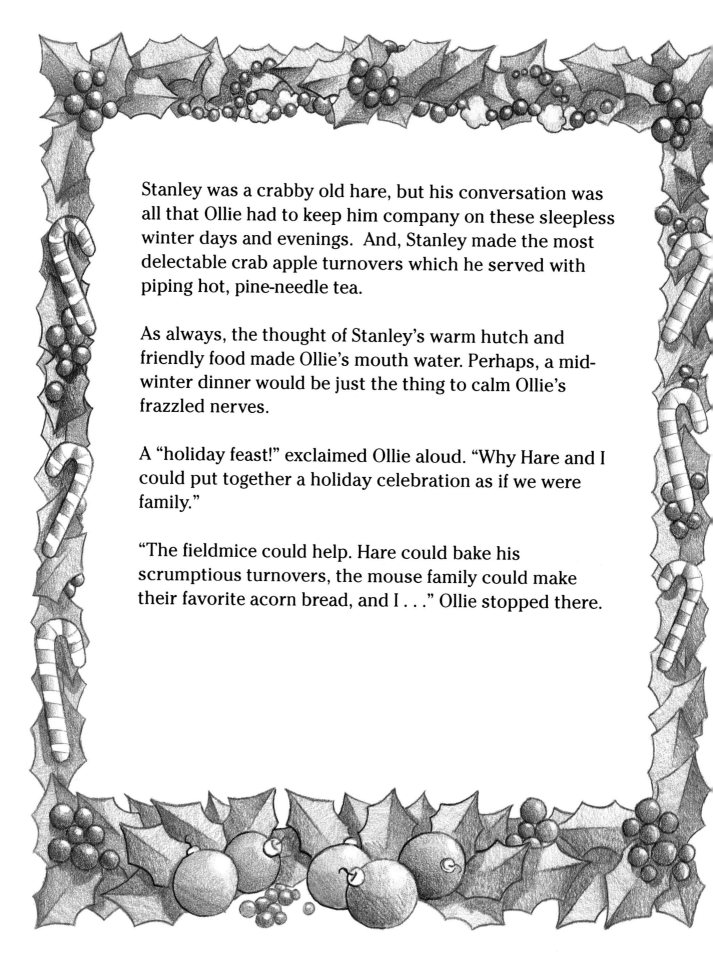

Stanley was a crabby old hare, but his conversation was all that Ollie had to keep him company on these sleepless winter days and evenings. And, Stanley made the most delectable crab apple turnovers which he served with piping hot, pine-needle tea.

As always, the thought of Stanley's warm hutch and friendly food made Ollie's mouth water. Perhaps, a mid-winter dinner would be just the thing to calm Ollie's frazzled nerves.

A "holiday feast!" exclaimed Ollie aloud. "Why Hare and I could put together a holiday celebration as if we were family."

"The fieldmice could help. Hare could bake his scrumptious turnovers, the mouse family could make their favorite acorn bread, and I . . ." Ollie stopped there.

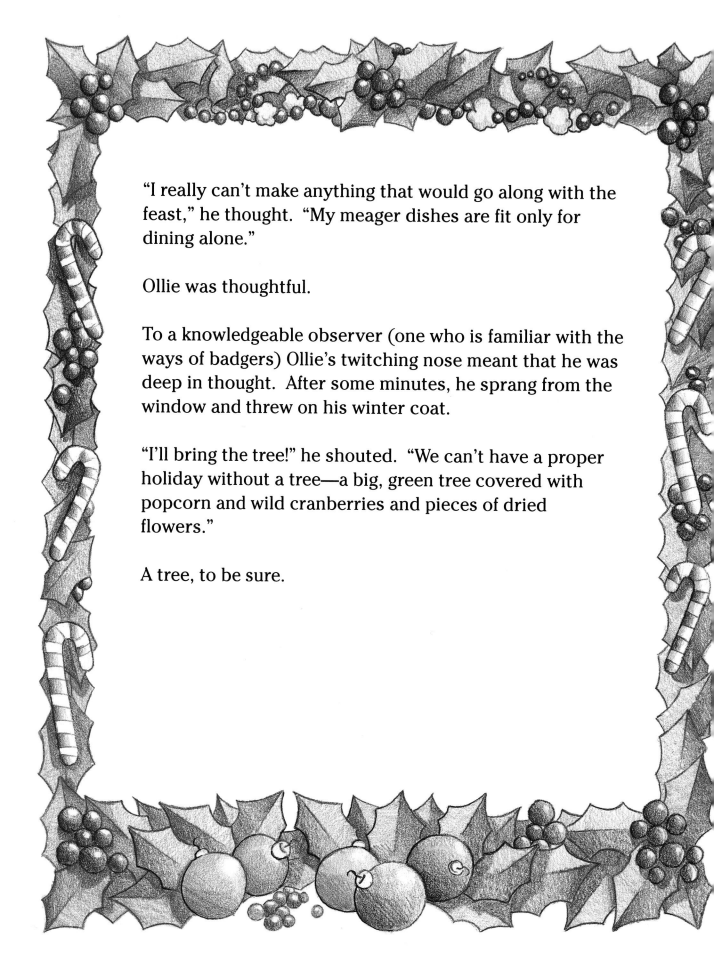

"I really can't make anything that would go along with the feast," he thought. "My meager dishes are fit only for dining alone."

Ollie was thoughtful.

To a knowledgeable observer (one who is familiar with the ways of badgers) Ollie's twitching nose meant that he was deep in thought. After some minutes, he sprang from the window and threw on his winter coat.

"I'll bring the tree!" he shouted. "We can't have a proper holiday without a tree—a big, green tree covered with popcorn and wild cranberries and pieces of dried flowers."

A tree, to be sure.

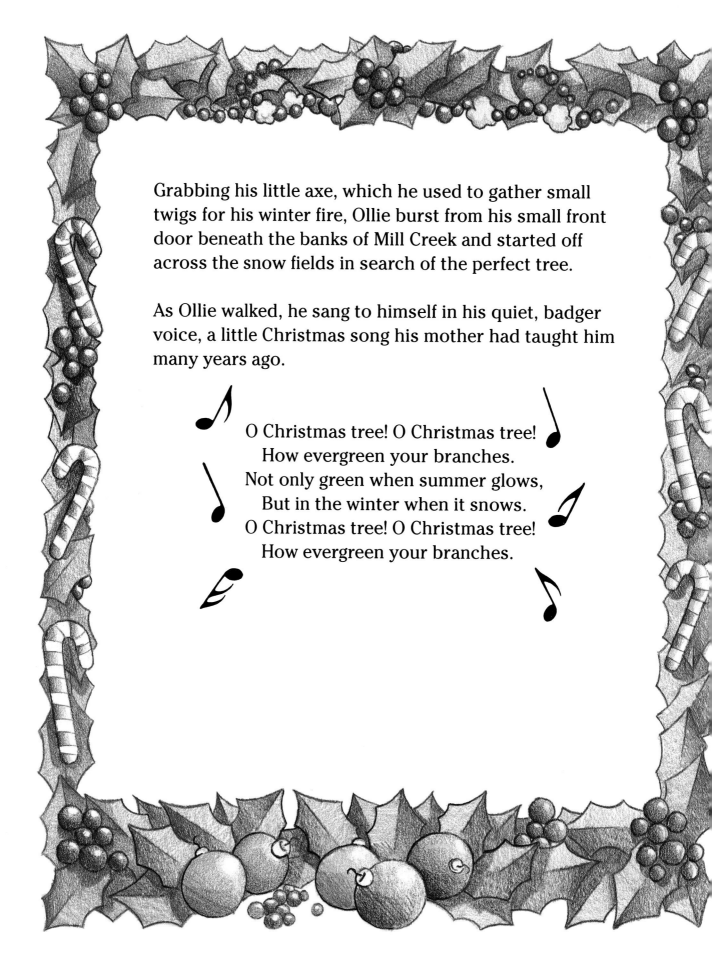

Grabbing his little axe, which he used to gather small twigs for his winter fire, Ollie burst from his small front door beneath the banks of Mill Creek and started off across the snow fields in search of the perfect tree.

As Ollie walked, he sang to himself in his quiet, badger voice, a little Christmas song his mother had taught him many years ago.

O Christmas tree! O Christmas tree!
   How evergreen your branches.
Not only green when summer glows,
   But in the winter when it snows.
O Christmas tree! O Christmas tree!
   How evergreen your branches.

Through the cold morning, Ollie searched for the perfect tree. He searched high and he searched low, but nowhere could he find a tree just right for his needs (that is, a tree small enough for a badger to cut down and carry through the woods to the hutch of Stanley Livingston Hare).

Ollie had just about decided that a party was not such a great idea after all when suddenly he spied, in the distance, the perfect tree.

It was small, about his own height, and it was the greenest tree he had ever seen. Ollie was wild with delight! He ran in his fastest badger fashion to the tree.

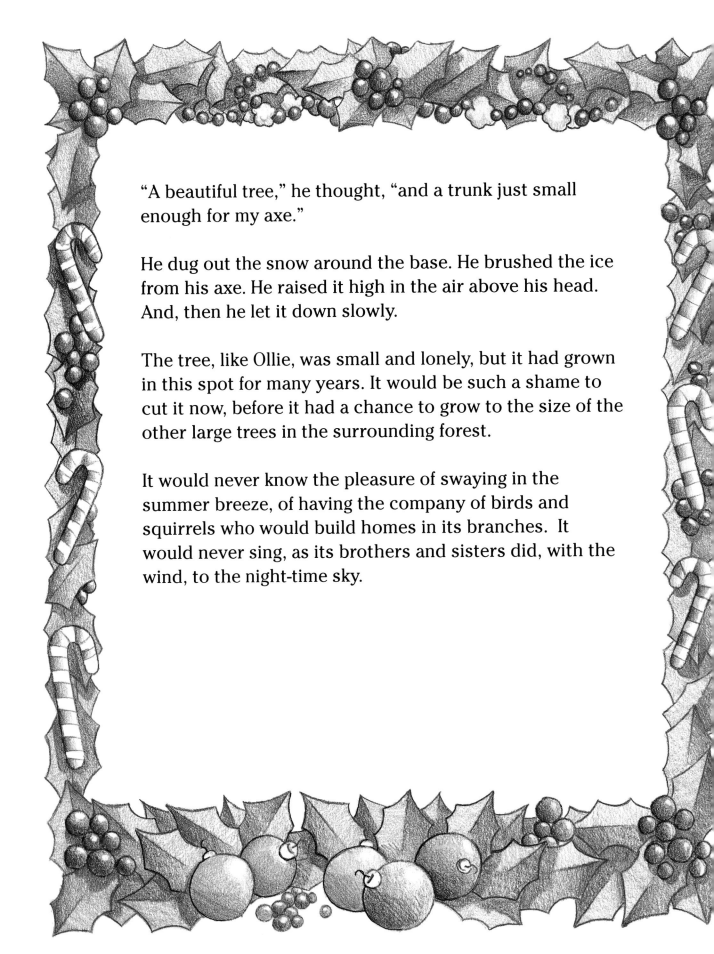

"A beautiful tree," he thought, "and a trunk just small enough for my axe."

He dug out the snow around the base. He brushed the ice from his axe. He raised it high in the air above his head. And, then he let it down slowly.

The tree, like Ollie, was small and lonely, but it had grown in this spot for many years. It would be such a shame to cut it now, before it had a chance to grow to the size of the other large trees in the surrounding forest.

It would never know the pleasure of swaying in the summer breeze, of having the company of birds and squirrels who would build homes in its branches. It would never sing, as its brothers and sisters did, with the wind, to the night-time sky.

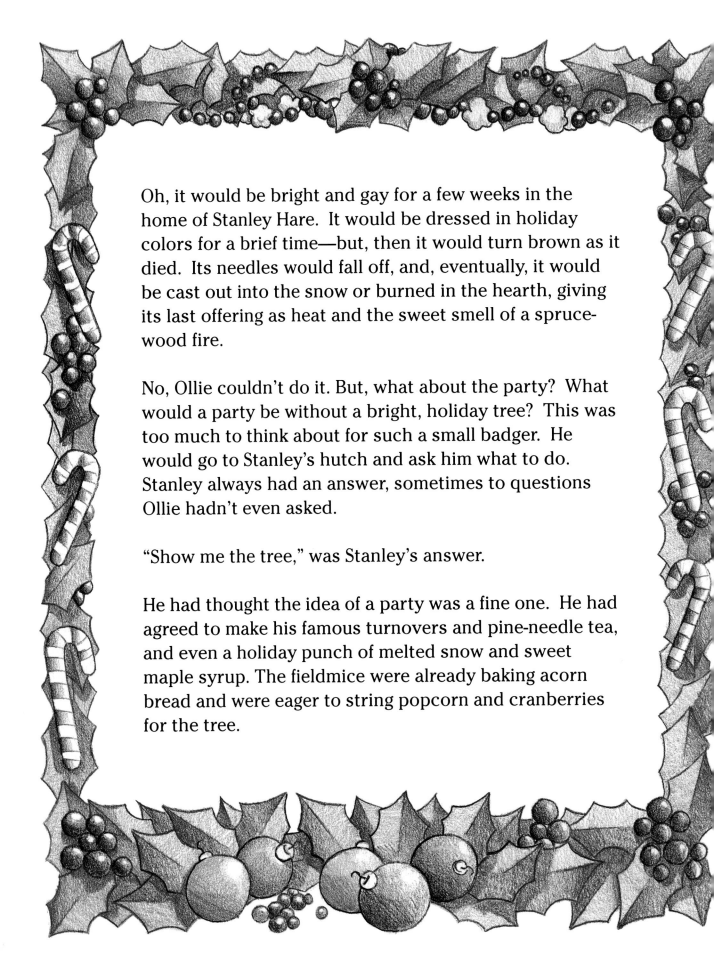

Oh, it would be bright and gay for a few weeks in the home of Stanley Hare. It would be dressed in holiday colors for a brief time—but, then it would turn brown as it died. Its needles would fall off, and, eventually, it would be cast out into the snow or burned in the hearth, giving its last offering as heat and the sweet smell of a spruce-wood fire.

No, Ollie couldn't do it. But, what about the party? What would a party be without a bright, holiday tree? This was too much to think about for such a small badger. He would go to Stanley's hutch and ask him what to do. Stanley always had an answer, sometimes to questions Ollie hadn't even asked.

"Show me the tree," was Stanley's answer.

He had thought the idea of a party was a fine one. He had agreed to make his famous turnovers and pine-needle tea, and even a holiday punch of melted snow and sweet maple syrup. The fieldmice were already baking acorn bread and were eager to string popcorn and cranberries for the tree.

But Stanley understood Ollie better than anyone, and if the lonely badger saw something special in the little tree, then he must also see it.

So, wrapped against the cold and accompanied by the fieldmouse father, the friends trudged off toward where Ollie's perfect tree grew.

"There it is!" cried Ollie, obviously excited again at the sight of such a perfect tree. And, sure enough, it was. Stanley agreed that it was the finest tree he had ever seen. The fieldmouse father scampered around the trunk in excitement, slipping on the ice and making loud, squeaky noises.

A fine tree indeed—so fine, in fact, that Ollie began to hum again, the song of the Christmas tree.

Soon his quiet hum was joined by Stanley Hare's strong voice; and, before long, the fieldmouse father added his squeaky sounds to the verse.

O Christmas tree! O Christmas tree!
How evergreen your branches.
Not only green when summer glows,
But in the winter when it snows.
O Christmas tree! O Christmas tree!
How evergreen your branches.

The words hung before them like their frosty breath for a moment, then disappeared into the winter air.

"You are right," said Stanley. "We cannot cut such a fine tree, even for our party. We must do without a tree."

Ollie's furry face grew long. "But, I so wanted to bring something to the party," he said. "You are all providing food and cheer, and I have nothing to bring but my hungry self. And what is a holiday party without a tree?"

Stanley thought for a long moment.

The day was rapidly drawing to a close. The moon could now be seen in the still, blue sky, and he knew that night was not far off. Of course, for most wild things, night was a time of activity, but there were still turnovers to bake and punch to make.

"We'll decorate it here," he said. "The fieldmouse family should be finished stringing the popcorn and cranberries by now. We will bring them to the tree and put them on here in the woods."

"What a splendid idea!" cried Ollie. "That way we won't have to cut it down, and we shall have a holiday tree after all!"

And so, in no time at all, they were decorating the small, green tree with all manner of festive dress. The fieldmouse family dragged the many ornaments they had made to the tree as Stanley and Ollie hung them on the branches.

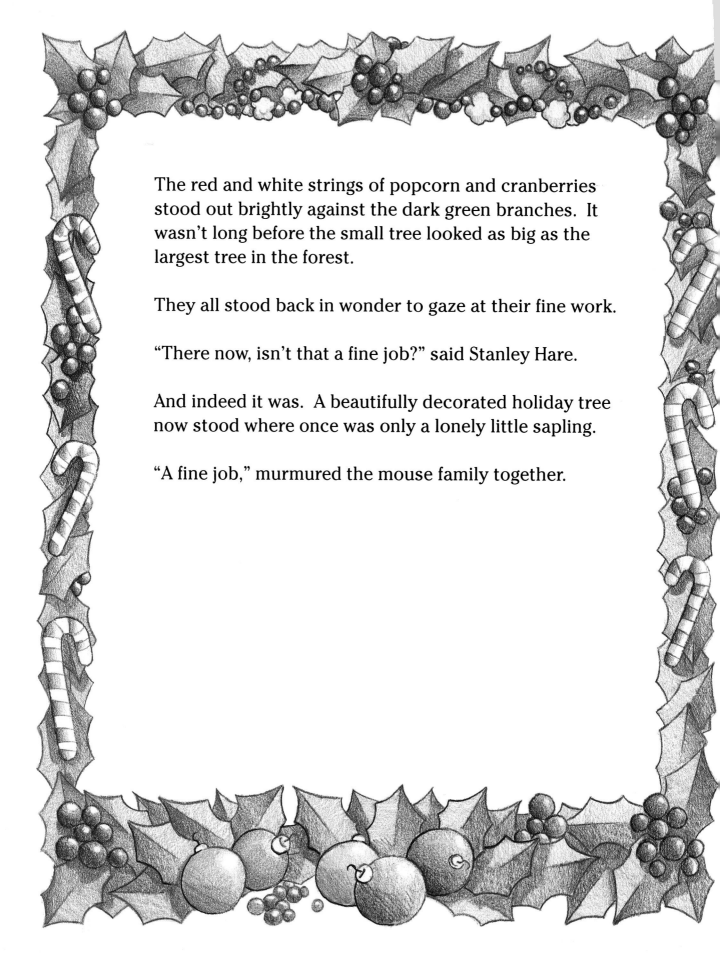

The red and white strings of popcorn and cranberries stood out brightly against the dark green branches. It wasn't long before the small tree looked as big as the largest tree in the forest.

They all stood back in wonder to gaze at their fine work.

"There now, isn't that a fine job?" said Stanley Hare.

And indeed it was. A beautifully decorated holiday tree now stood where once was only a lonely little sapling.

"A fine job," murmured the mouse family together.

In the quiet of the moment, Stanley began to sing. It was a song so soft that it seemed to become a part of the dark, quiet forest itself.

Silent night, holy night,
    All is calm. All is bright.
'Round yon Virgin, mother and child.
    Holy infant, so tender and mild.
Sleep in heavenly peace.
Sleep in heavenly peace.

The friends stood for a while admiring their work, then Stanley said, "We have our tree, but our meal is still to be made, and it is very far from here to my house. We had better be going if we are to have a feast tonight."

Ollie knew that he was right, but he hated to leave his lovely tree so soon.

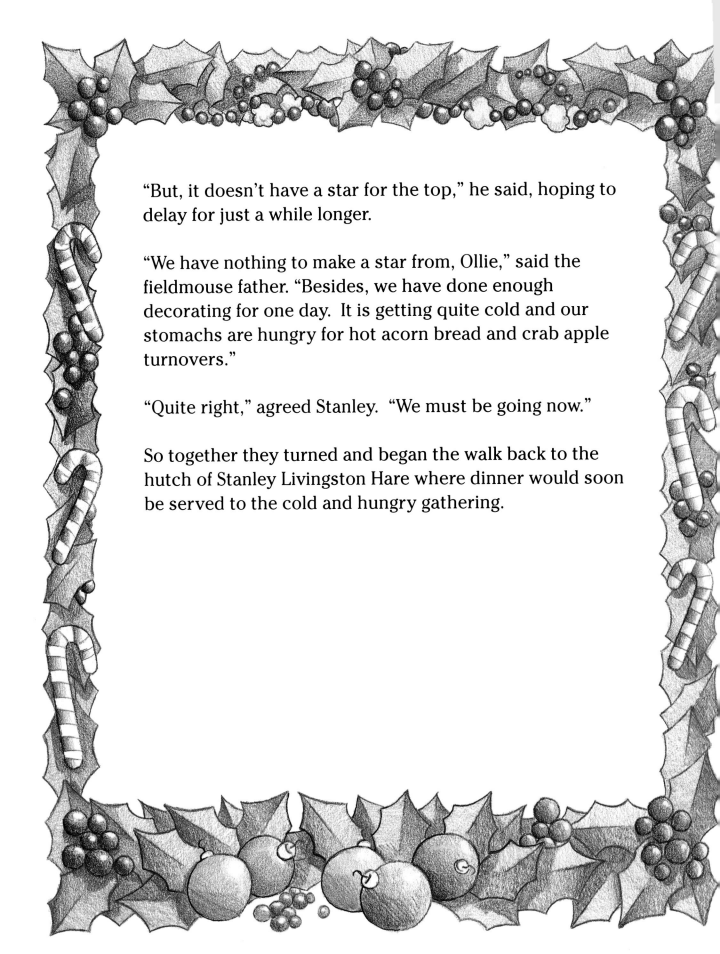

"But, it doesn't have a star for the top," he said, hoping to delay for just a while longer.

"We have nothing to make a star from, Ollie," said the fieldmouse father. "Besides, we have done enough decorating for one day. It is getting quite cold and our stomachs are hungry for hot acorn bread and crab apple turnovers."

"Quite right," agreed Stanley. "We must be going now."

So together they turned and began the walk back to the hutch of Stanley Livingston Hare where dinner would soon be served to the cold and hungry gathering.

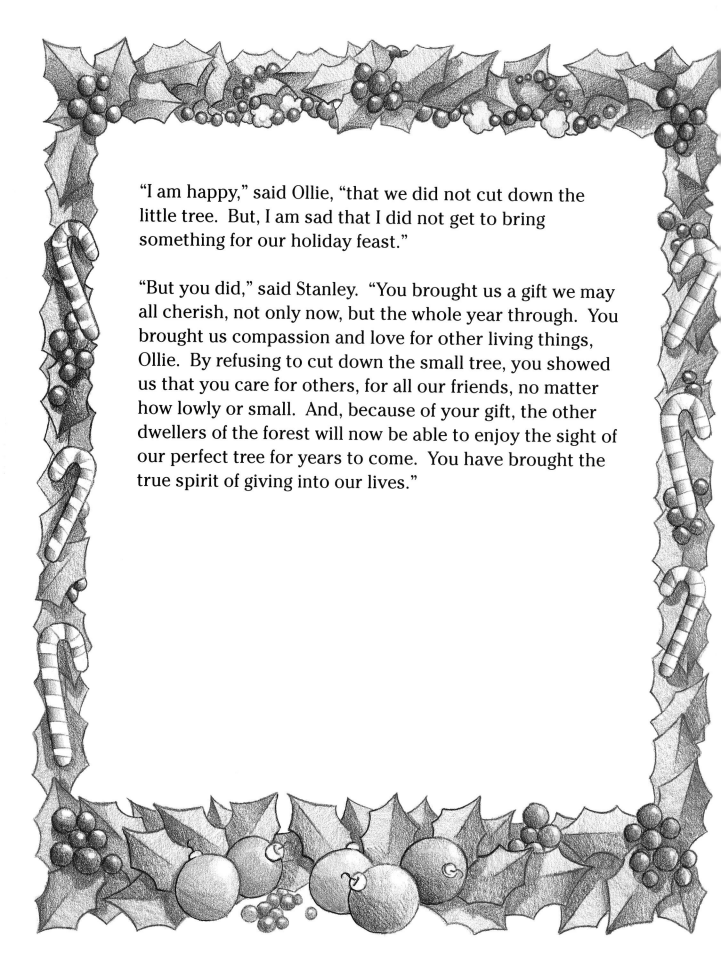

"I am happy," said Ollie, "that we did not cut down the little tree. But, I am sad that I did not get to bring something for our holiday feast."

"But you did," said Stanley. "You brought us a gift we may all cherish, not only now, but the whole year through. You brought us compassion and love for other living things, Ollie. By refusing to cut down the small tree, you showed us that you care for others, for all our friends, no matter how lowly or small. And, because of your gift, the other dwellers of the forest will now be able to enjoy the sight of our perfect tree for years to come. You have brought the true spirit of giving into our lives."

Despite the cold, Ollie felt warm inside.

As they reached the edge of the clearing and were about to pass into the woods toward the house of Stanley Livingston Hare, they turned to have one, last look at their perfect tree.

It still stood, as it would for many years to come, dark green against a fading day, whispering softly in the winter wind.

And, as they watched, the evening star rose behind it and came to rest, for a brief, shining moment, above its crown.

For over a decade, Unicorn has been publishing
richly illustrated editions of classic and contemporary works
for children and adults. To continue this tradition,
WE WOULD LIKE TO KNOW WHAT YOU THINK.

If you would like to send us your suggestions or obtain
a list of our current titles, please write to:
THE UNICORN PUBLISHING HOUSE, INC.
P.O. Box 377
Morris Plains, NJ 07950
ATT: Dept CLP

❖❖❖❖

Printing History 15 14 13 12 11 10 9 8 7 6 5 4 3 2 1

Library of Congress Cataloging-in-Publication Data

Bivins, Thomas Harvey, 1947-
    The Perfect Tree and Favorite Christmas Carols / story by Thomas
Bivins; illustrated by Christopher Bivins.
    p. cm. — (Through the Magic Window)
    Summary: Badger sets out to find the perfect Christmas tree but is
reluctant to destroy the tree's beauty by cutting it down. Includes
three traditional Christmas carols.
    ISBN 0-88101-104-5
    [1. Christmas—Fiction. 2. Christmas trees—Fiction. 3. Trees—
Fiction. 4. Badgers—Fiction. 5. Carols. 6. Christmas music.] I. Bivins,
Christopher, 1961- ill. II. Title. III. Series.
    PZ7.B52855Pe 1990
    [E]—dc20   90-34514
                                                                CIP
                                                                AC

To Lonnie,
for whom the story was written
as a Christmas gift many years ago,
and to Joni.

Oliver Wendel Badger &
Stanley Livingston Hare are
both modeled after their
real counterparts who lived along
the banks of Mill Creek and who
frequently dined on the fallen fruit of
our crab apple tree.

It Came Upon
a Midnight Clear

It came upon a midnight clear,
That glorious song of old,
From angels bending near the earth
To touch their harps of gold.

Peace on the earth, good will to men
From heaven's all gracious King.
The world in solemn stillness lay
To hear the angels sing.